T0365000

Goodbye Buddy

"Honoring the Unbreakable Bond: A Journey Through Pet Loss, The Death Process, and Healing."

A. M. Ford

Goodbye Buddy

"HONORING THE UNBREAKABLE BOND: A JOURNEY THROUGH PET LOSS, THE DEATH PROCESS, AND HEALING."

iUniverse books may be ordered through booksellers or by contacting:

iUniverse
1663 Liberty Drive
Bloomington, IN 47403
www.iuniverse.com
844-349-9409

ISBN: 978-1-6632-6725-2 (sc)
ISBN: 978-1-6632-6800-6 (hc)
ISBN: 978-1-6632-6724-5 (e)

Library of Congress Control Number: 2024920751

Print information available on the last page.

iUniverse rev. date: 10/11/2024

Goodbye

Buddy

Today, I was told I have to say goodbye to my closest friend, my fierce protector, my beloved dog, Buddy.

Words can't express the love and loyalty he has given me over the years. He has been by my side through thick and thin, always with unwavering devotion. My heart aches knowing I must let him go.

3

Buddy has been a part of my life for as long as I can remember. In fact, there isn't a memory without him.

He is so much more than a dog. He is an irreplaceable member of this family. And I can't imagine my world without Buddy in it.

Buddy was my parents' first baby. He was only a year old when I was born, so we basically grew up together. Buddy has been more than just a dog to me—he's been my constant companion and a true member of our family.

He was there when I took my first steps, always catching my fall. He taught me how to swim, even though I mostly used him as a flotation device in the pool.

Buddy was my favorite ball player; we could play catch for hours. And it was Buddy who gave me the confidence to ride my bike without training wheels.

Growing up together, he has been by my side through it all, and I can't imagine my life without him.

Buddy even helped me lose my very first tooth! We tied a piece of string from my wiggly tooth to his collar and tossed a ball across the room. Buddy, ever excited, took off to fetch it, and my tooth came right out. We never found that tooth, but it happened so quickly that it didn't even hurt.

I found a love for books after learning to read to Buddy. He enjoyed our story times and listened so attentively. He was my secret keeper, the one I told everything to, and the one who comforted me after my first heartbreak.

At the beginning of fourth grade, Lucy Parker dumped me for the new kid in school, and I thought I would never get over it. Thank goodness I had Buddy to console me during that tough time.

Buddy was always by my side, and wherever I went, he followed. We cherished our walks along the trails in the woods behind my house and loved exploring the outdoors together. From catching crawfish and salamanders in the creek to him pushing me on the old rope swing, our adventures were always filled with joy. Buddy wasn't just a dog; he was my best friend.

I'll never forget the day Buddy saved me after I fell out of a tree. They say dogs have a sixth sense, and Buddy must have had an intuition that day. He barked at me the entire time I climbed, growing louder with each branch I scaled. He even tried pulling at my shirt to stop me from going any higher. Of course, I didn't listen and climbed until I fell, breaking my first bone. In my pain, I couldn't walk, but Buddy, though reluctant to leave my side, ran off to get help. His bravery and loyalty in that moment were beyond words.

That summer was one of the hardest I've ever faced. With my leg in a cast, I couldn't go swimming, play sports, or see any of my friends. It felt like everything I enjoyed was out of reach. Thankfully, I had Buddy by my side. His companionship made even the toughest days a little more bearable.

However, that was the summer I met Paige. Our paths crossed because Buddy wanted to play with her dog, Chloe. Despite the challenges, Buddy led me to a new friend, and that connection was a bright spot in an otherwise difficult time.

Paige is now one of my closest friends, and we just went to our first middle school dance together. Buddy was there to send me off on my first real date, and he was there waiting for me to tell him all about it once I returned home.

Buddy has been a part of so many memories and major milestones in my life. Through every joy and challenge, he's been a constant source of comfort. Tonight, will be the last night he sleeps in my bed and the last time I get to hold him while I fall asleep.

Tomorrow, I'll have to find the courage to say goodbye.

23

Today I must do one of the hardest things I have ever had to face- saying goodbye to my best friend, Buddy.

I've never experienced death before, the hardest reality about this, is knowing I'm not going to see him again. He's old now, 15 and can't run or play like he used to. He struggles to get around, and lately, he hasn't had much of an appetite. I want to do the right thing for him, but my heart just isn't ready to say goodbye.

My parents say that it would be selfish to keep Buddy any longer because he's in pain and doesn't have the same quality of life he once did. The right thing to do is to let him go, to free him from sickness and old age. I know this will give him peace and take away his pain, but it's so hard to face. Letting him go is the last thing I want to do, but it's what's best for my sweet Buddy.

Part of me doesn't want to make this decision, but I also don't want to be selfish. I love Buddy with every piece of my heart, and there's nothing I wouldn't do to take away his pain. But I don't know if I'm ready for this. My mom reminded me that we could never truly be ready, that death never gets easier, and we're going to be sad for a while. But if we love Buddy, we shouldn't want him to struggle anymore, and the best thing we can do for him is to let him go.

I held my boy close and knew I had to be strong for him. I fought back the tears and made the decision to do what was best for Buddy. Even though I didn't fully understand what would happen next, I knew my faithful pup needed me, and I would be there for him through this difficult time. He wouldn't have to go through this alone.

When we arrived at the vet, Buddy was understandably stressed and nervous. I tried my best to comfort him, just as he's always been there for me. When the doctor walked in, I couldn't help but ask again if there was truly no other option for Buddy. Wasn't there something else we could do for him?

The vet explained that we've done everything possible to help Buddy, but unfortunately, he isn't getting any better. As animals age, their bodies stop working properly, and Buddy's quality of life has deteriorated. His organs were beginning to shut down, and the kindest thing we could do now was to alleviate his pain and help him pass peacefully with euthanasia.

I didn't know what euthanasia was and was deeply concerned about what would happen next. The doctor reassured me that it would not hurt, and that Buddy wouldn't be scared. She explained that she would first give him medicine to help him relax, and then a special shot to gently stop his heart. Buddy would fall asleep peacefully and wouldn't feel any pain.

The doctor gave us all the time we needed to say our final goodbyes, but I was still in disbelief that this moment had come. I couldn't accept that I would never hold my boy again, play catch with him, or share my secrets.

The finality of it all was almost too much to bear. When the time came to say goodbye, I struggled to find the words to express how much he meant to me, how much joy he brought into my life, and how nothing would ever be the same without him.

Once we were ready, we discussed what to do with Buddy. I couldn't bear the thought of burying him in the ground or leaving him behind. The doctor suggested having him cremated with Heavenly Gates Pet Cremation, so that Buddy could come home with us.

Arrangements were made for Buddy to be picked up by this wonderful company that truly loves animals. They treat each pet with the respect and dignity that my precious boy deserved. Knowing Buddy was in caring hands gave me some comfort during this heartbreaking time.

HEAVENLY GATES

PET CREMATION

When we met with the staff from Heavenly Gates, I asked what cremation was since I had never heard of it before. They explained that it's the process of reducing a deceased pet's body to ashes using high heat. It's a respectful and dignified way to handle your pet's remains, allowing them to return home to you after the process was completed.

We opted for a private cremation, which means Buddy was cremated alone, and his ashes will be returned to us. Afterward, we can choose to scatter his ashes in a special place or keep them in a memorial urn. The process is handled with the utmost care and respect, ensuring that Buddy's remains are treated with compassion. Knowing this brings some peace during such a painful time.

Heavenly Gates Pet Cremation was amazing during this difficult time. They never treated us like customers; they truly understood our struggle. They were patient while we made our decisions and incredibly supportive with everything we needed. I felt at peace knowing Buddy was in the best possible hands, and it gave us some relief and comfort to have him come back home with us.

For days, or maybe even weeks, I cried. The house felt so empty without Buddy greeting me. I felt incredibly lonely without him and would give anything just to see him again. I try to remind myself that he is in a better place now, no longer suffering.

Still, Buddy has left a huge void in my life and what feels like a gaping hole in my heart.

Even though it's been a couple of months since Buddy passed, I'm still heartbroken over his absence. My family thinks it might be time to get another dog. At first, I thought this was the absolute worst idea. Part of me never wants to love another dog because I fear experiencing that kind of pain and heartache again. I also worry that getting another dog would feel like replacing Buddy, and I could never love another pup as much as I loved him. Buddy was the greatest dog there ever was, and he will never be replaced.

My mom agreed and reassured me that Buddy would never be replaced. He was truly one of a kind, and there will never be another dog like him. She explained that getting a new dog doesn't replace the old one; it simply expands your heart. A new puppy could provide a welcome distraction from the void Buddy left behind, without ever diminishing the love and memory of the one we lost.

We eventually adopted a new puppy and named her Lily. She's adorable and a bit of a handful, and while she's growing on me, nothing can ever replace my pal, Buddy. I still miss him terribly, and not a day goes by without thinking about and missing him.

However, having Lily around has made things a little easier, and it's been nice having a dog in the house again.

About the Author

A. M. Ford is a passionate animal lover, lifelong advocate for pets, and dedicated pet care professional. With years of experience working in the pet care industry, Amy has been committed to helping animals and supporting pet owners through all stages of their pet's lives. Surrounded by her own beloved pets, she understands the  deep bond between humans and animals, which inspired her to write her first book, a heartfelt story on pet loss for children. Through her work, Amy strives to provide comfort and guidance to those navigating the difficult emotions of saying goodbye to a beloved companion.